The Little Book of Joyous Thoughts

ANGEL FINGERPRINTS
The Little Book of Joyous Thoughts

By Sharon Warren   Art by Elsie Petrequin
Copyright © 1995 by Sharon Warren All Rights Reserved
Title inspired by a quote from Carlos Santana, NBC, Oct 1994
For information address:
IMAGIC Unlimited   P.O. Box 779   Sedona, AZ 86339
1-800-945-4453
FIRST EDITION 2nd Printing
ISBN: 0-9636074-4-8
Library of Congress Catalog Card Number: 94-96699
1. Epigrams 2. Life - Quotations, maxims, etc. 3. Love - Quotations, maxims, etc.
I. Petrequin, Elsie. II. Title.
PN1441.W37.A54 1995   94-9669
808'.882-dc20
Printed in THE UNITED STATES OF AMERICA
10 9 8 7 6 5 4 3
Printed on Recycled paper

ANGEL FINGERPRINTS
The Little Book of Joyous Thoughts
by Sharon Warren

Cover design by Elsie Petrequin
Art & Calligraphy by Elsie Petrequin

Other books by Sharon Warren
& Elsie Petrequin

ONE LIGHT ONE LOVE
LONG LONG AGO

Music CD by Michael McCabe
& Sharon Warren

ONE LIGHT ONE LOVE, Vol. I

For information call: (800) 945-4453

"All of us carry a lot of pain. Healing means
to be whole and sound...that's my job...I work with
sound...so we heal people. I believe in my heart
that angels today...what they long for the most is for
us to have more compassion. When you do something
for the Highest Good for all people, those are
the **fingerprints that Angels leave behind.**"

quote by Carlos Santana
ANGELS II: Beyond The Light, NBC - Oct. 1994

Special thanks to Keith Johannessen,
Elsie Petrequin, Carol Guthrie Sjolander, Cheryl Long
Riffle, Steve Vaile, Colette DeWitt, Janet Holbrook and
all the friends who believe in me and in my vision of
this little book of joyous thoughts.

To my brothers
John, Gerald, and Howard Jr.

In loving memory of my father
Howard A. Smith

I will find happiness when I give to others what I most want for myself ... Love, acceptance, peace, tolerance, freedom.

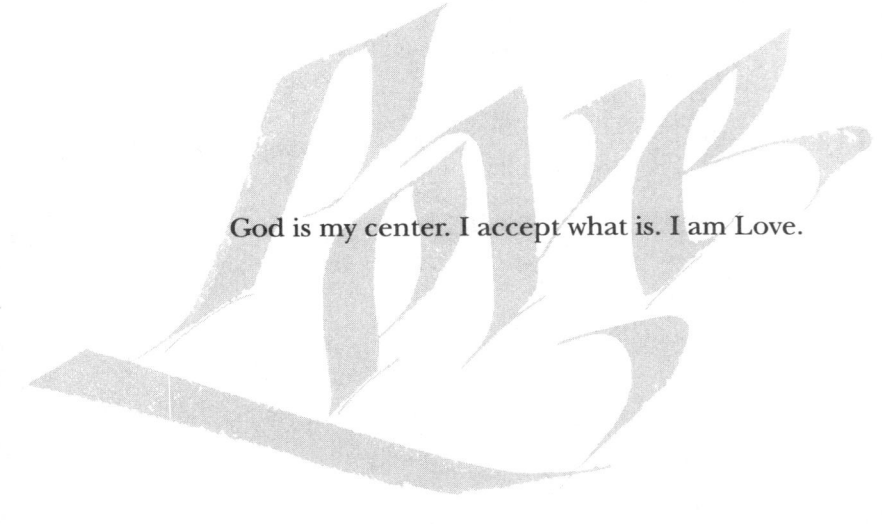

God is my center. I accept what is. I am Love.

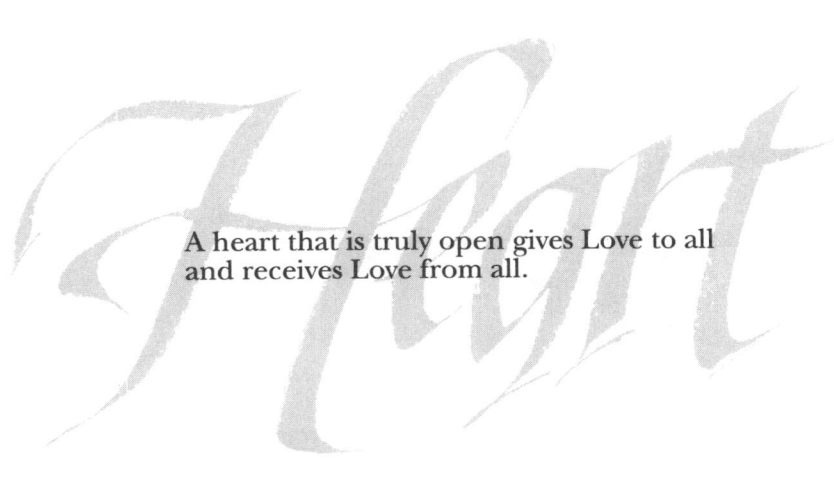

A heart that is truly open gives Love to all
and receives Love from all.

Trust him ... love him ... be strong and independent.
Ask nothing of him ... give him all the Love you feel
in your heart. That is your reward ... to give Love.

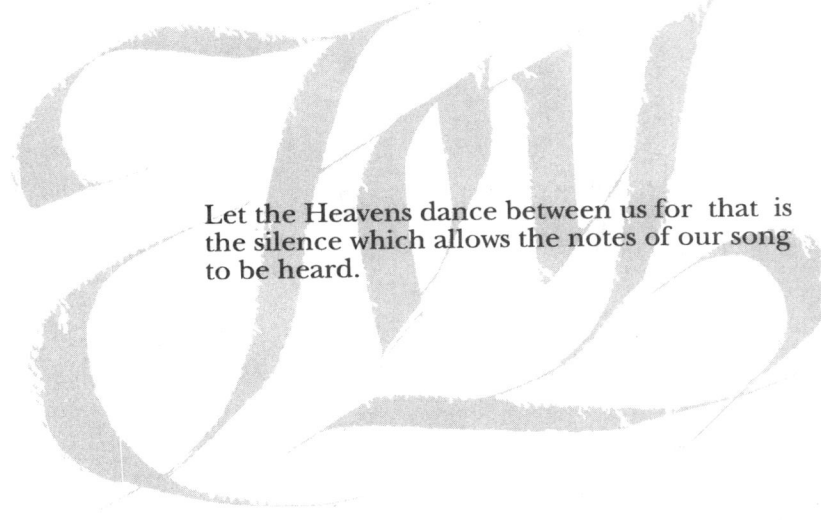

Let the Heavens dance between us for that is the silence which allows the notes of our song to be heard.

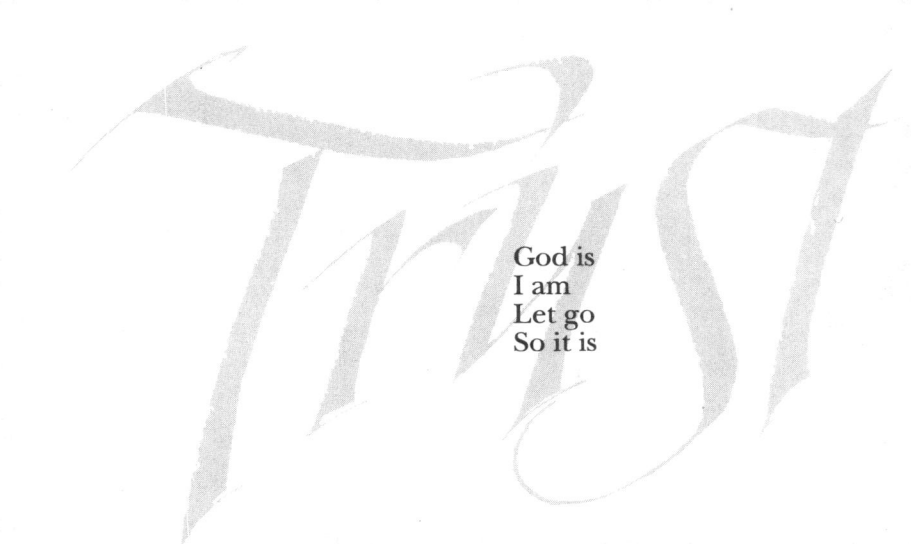

God is
I am
Let go
So it is

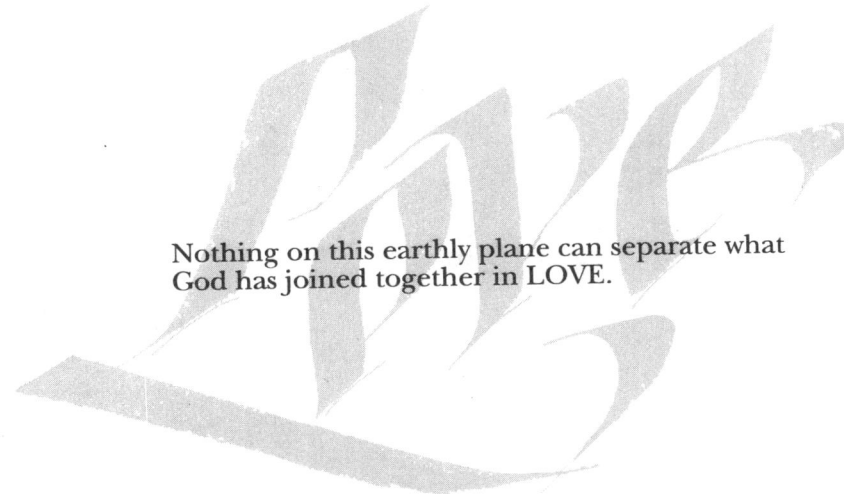

Nothing on this earthly plane can separate what God has joined together in LOVE.

I savor the memories of yesterday and live in the now of my existence.

True, pure, unconditional Love never dies.

Dreams

Let me hold you in my heart, my soul, and in my dreams ... experiencing you in my mind. For loving you has given me the power to know who I really am.

Safely surrounded by the peace of His tender Love,
I drift in a sea of warm, velvet sound of a summer
breeze.

Dreams

Great Spirit, grant that our hearts may always be young and our dreams may last forever.

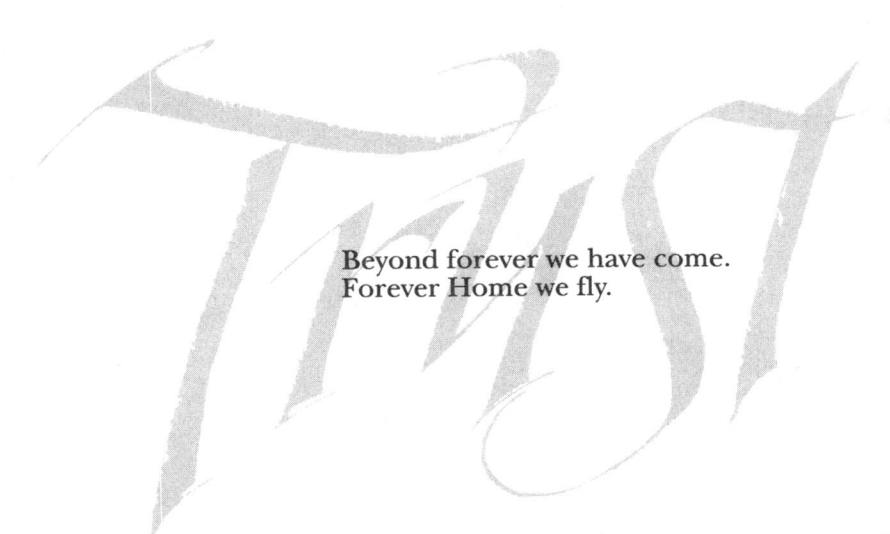

Trust

Beyond forever we have come.
Forever Home we fly.

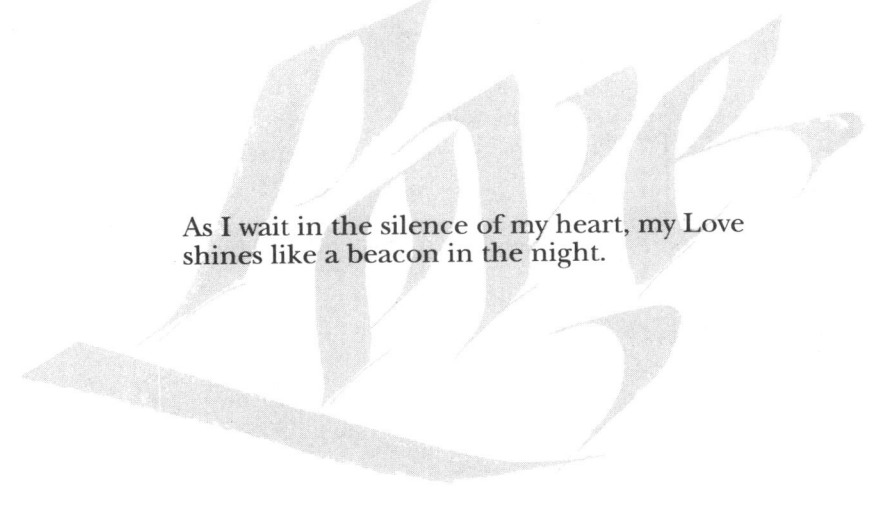

As I wait in the silence of my heart, my Love shines like a beacon in the night.

Light

You are all Light and all Love and all embracing.
You create nothing but good.

Love sustains us on life's turbulent waters.

You are wonderful! You bring out the best in people, and they bring out the best in you.

Energy

The energy is flowing, you bring me so much joy.

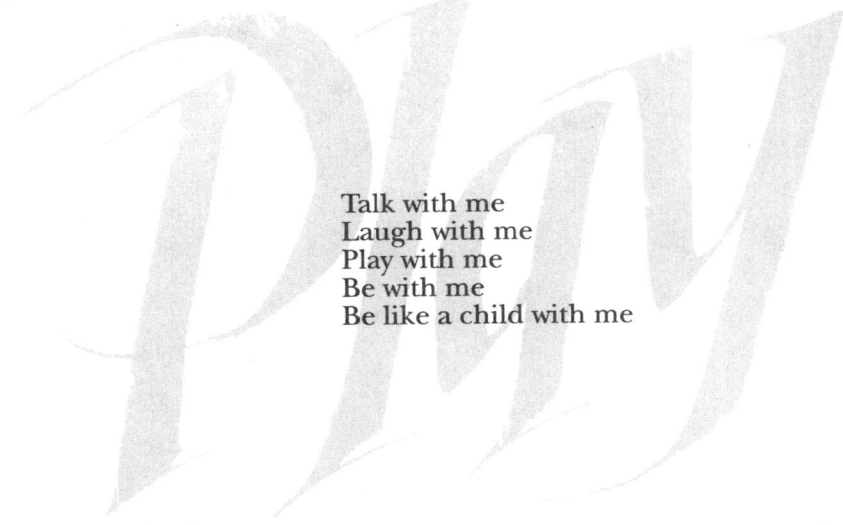

Talk with me
Laugh with me
Play with me
Be with me
Be like a child with me

The moon that you gaze upon shines down on me.

You are a little girl in a beautiful flower garden.
There are no spiders in your garden.

Light

You are gold. You are shining. You are brilliant.

Rest your heart on My shore.

You are becoming a diamond! A beautiful, clear, light-gathering and reflective, multi-faceted person, full of fire and brilliance.

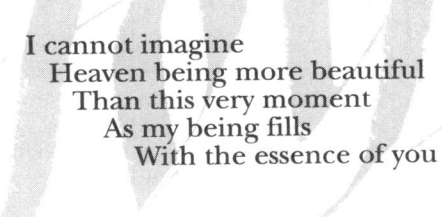

I cannot imagine
  Heaven being more beautiful
    Than this very moment
     As my being fills
       With the essence of you

You are beautiful,
You are loved.

Together two hearts beat as one ... born of Love, Eternal Love.

Light

You are a diamond ... I am one too!
Facet-nating and brilliant!

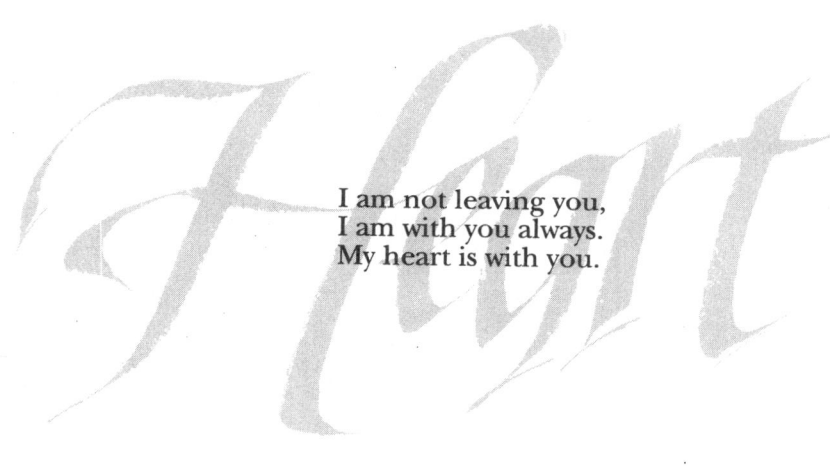

I am not leaving you,
I am with you always.
My heart is with you.

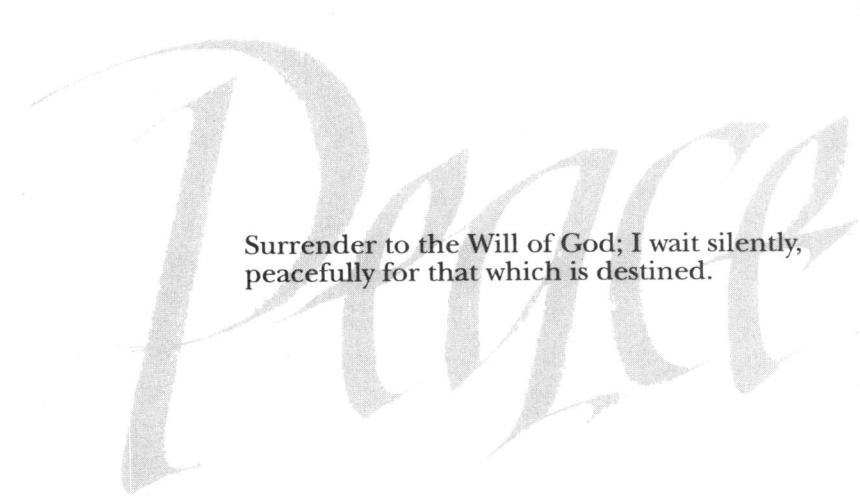

Surrender to the Will of God; I wait silently, peacefully for that which is destined.

Human

It's OK to make mistakes, 'cause we're only human, after all.

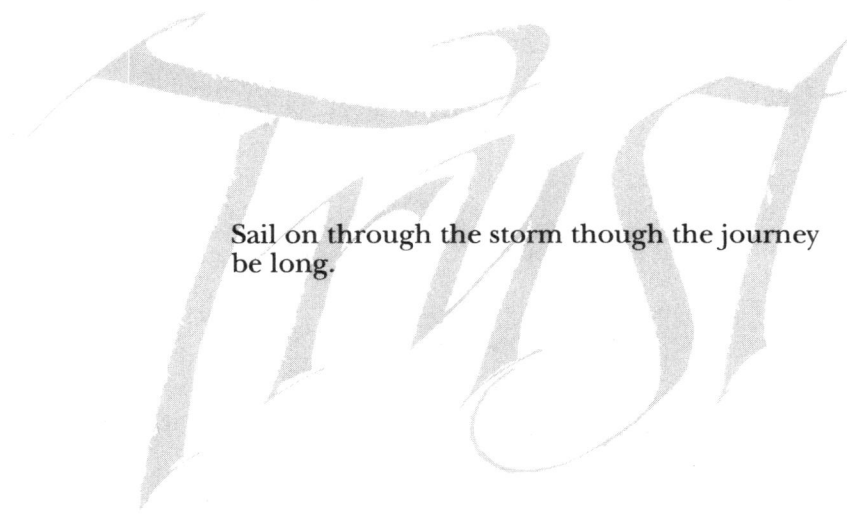

Sail on through the storm though the journey be long.

Remain human, for in all our frailties we find
lessons in life and appreciation for living.

Trust

Trust in Divine Order ... Let Go ... Relax ...
Everything is going to be fine!

In the center of the storm is the calm. Move with the storm ... have faith and let go of those things you can't control.

Only the illusion of time and space separates our two hearts.

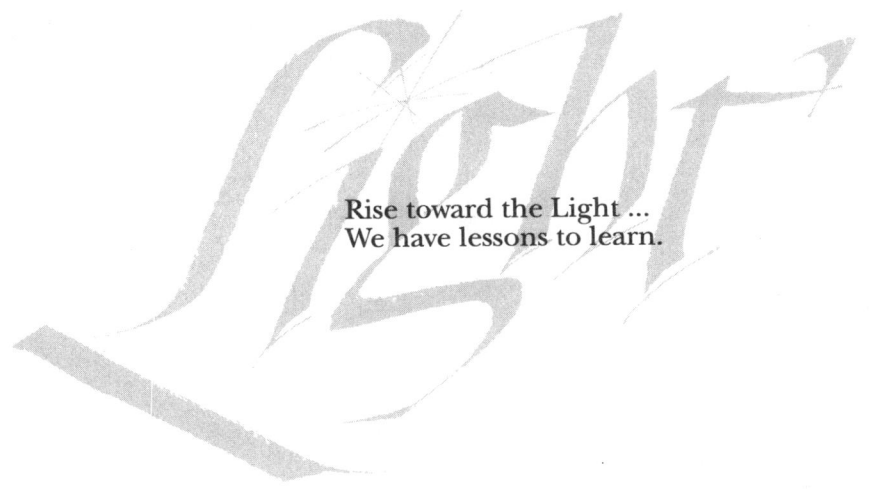

Rise toward the Light ...
We have lessons to learn.

Each moment is a MIRACLE! Embrace the miracle and the wonder of life.

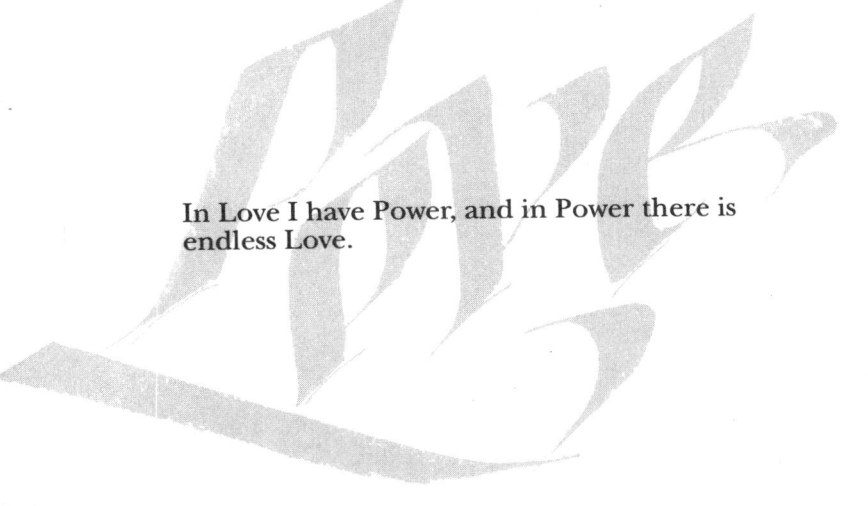

In Love I have Power, and in Power there is endless Love.

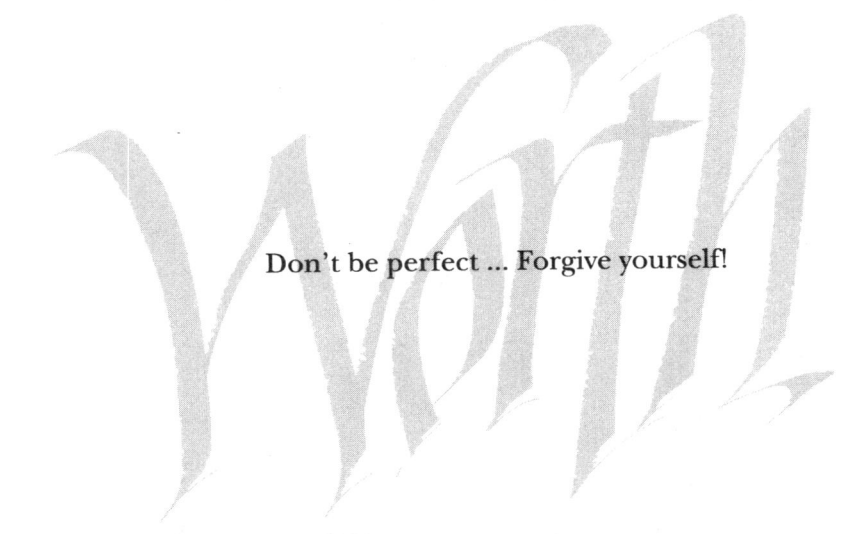
Don't be perfect ... Forgive yourself!

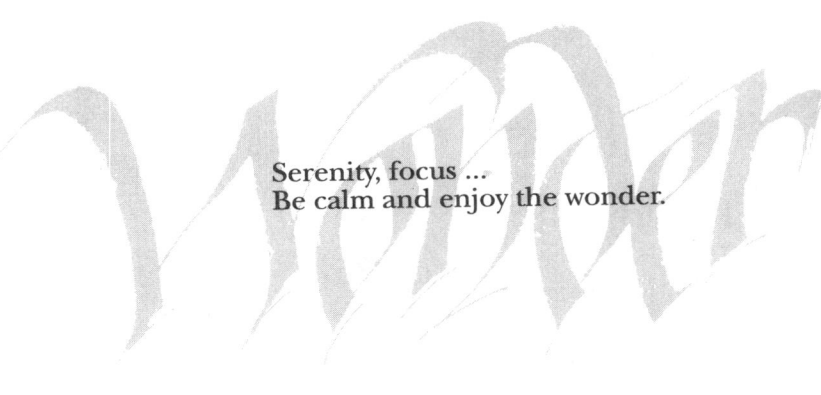

Serenity, focus ...
Be calm and enjoy the wonder.

What is magical shall never pass away, be your own magician, create your illusions to then make your own reality.

A woman's worth is infinite and is found within, a man's worth is boundless and is expressed without.

Magic

I create fulfilling magical relationships, where imagination, together with illusion, instill real feelings of intimacy.

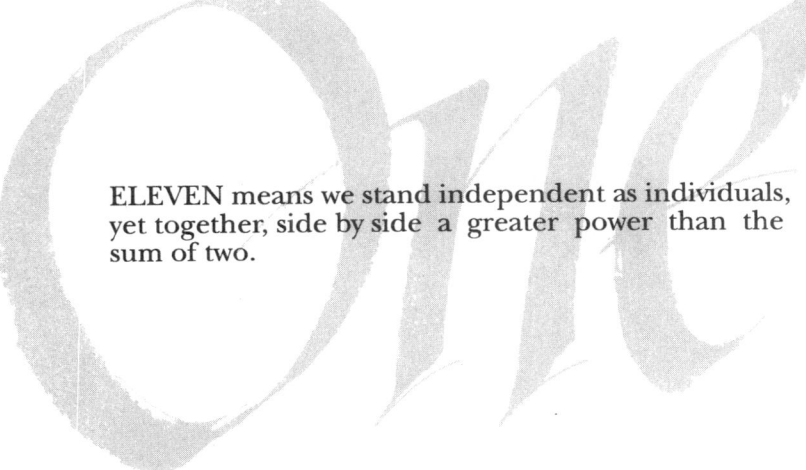

ELEVEN means we stand independent as individuals, yet together, side by side a greater power than the sum of two.

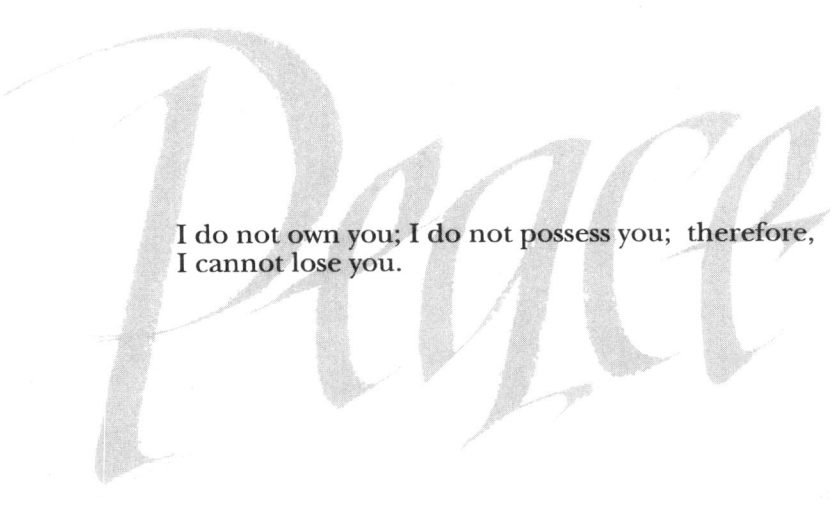

I do not own you; I do not possess you; therefore, I cannot lose you.

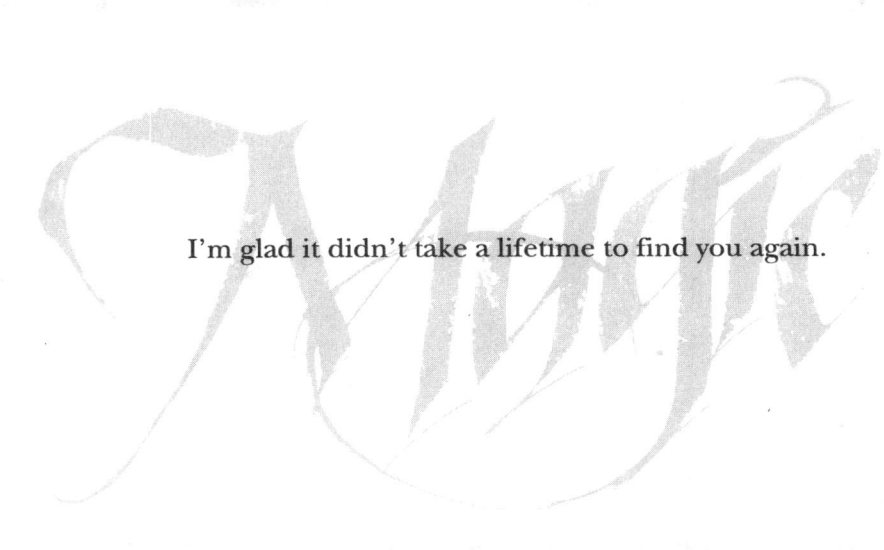

I'm glad it didn't take a lifetime to find you again.

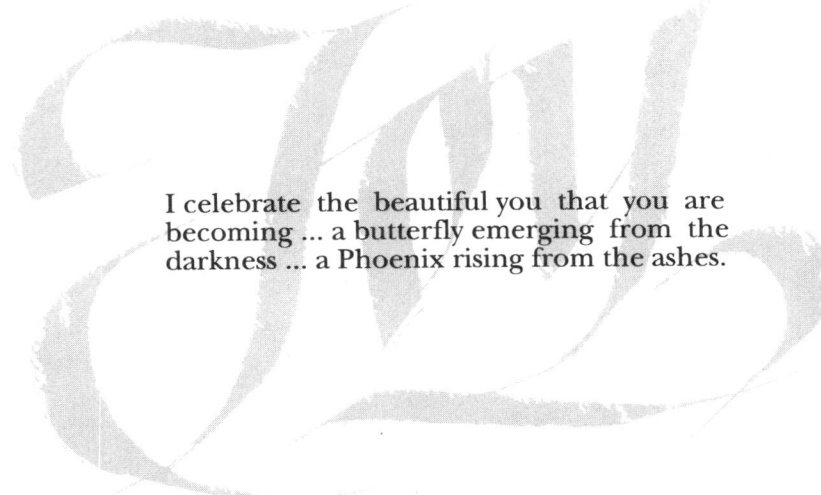

I celebrate the beautiful you that you are becoming ... a butterfly emerging from the darkness ... a Phoenix rising from the ashes.

I love every nuance of you.

I see the precious you that you have always been.

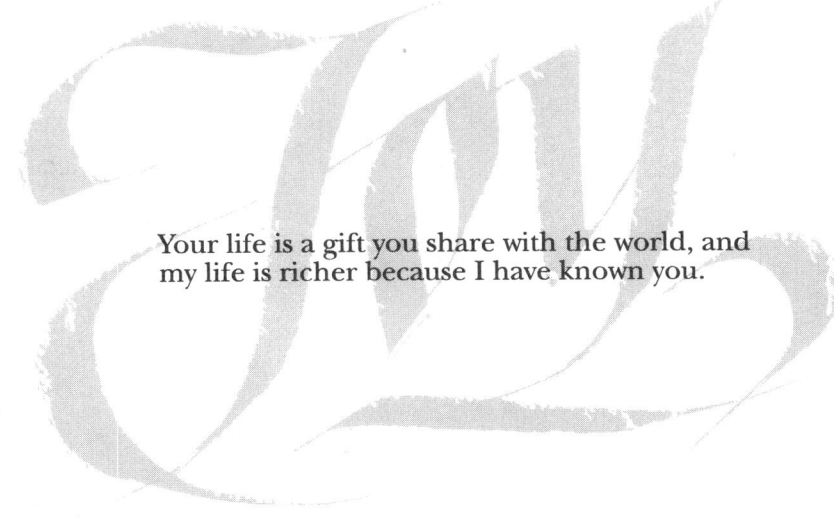

Your life is a gift you share with the world, and my life is richer because I have known you.

Our spirits fly so high ...
Each day of life is a miracle ...
We are One Light One Love.

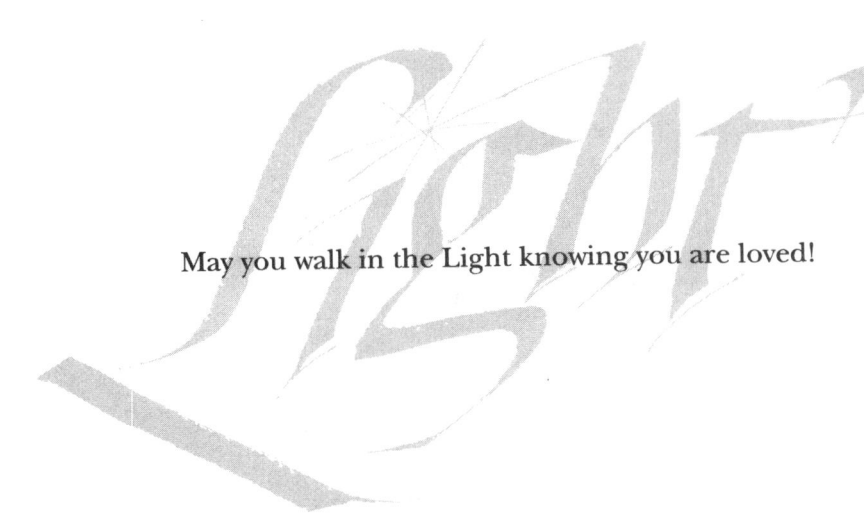

May you walk in the Light knowing you are loved!

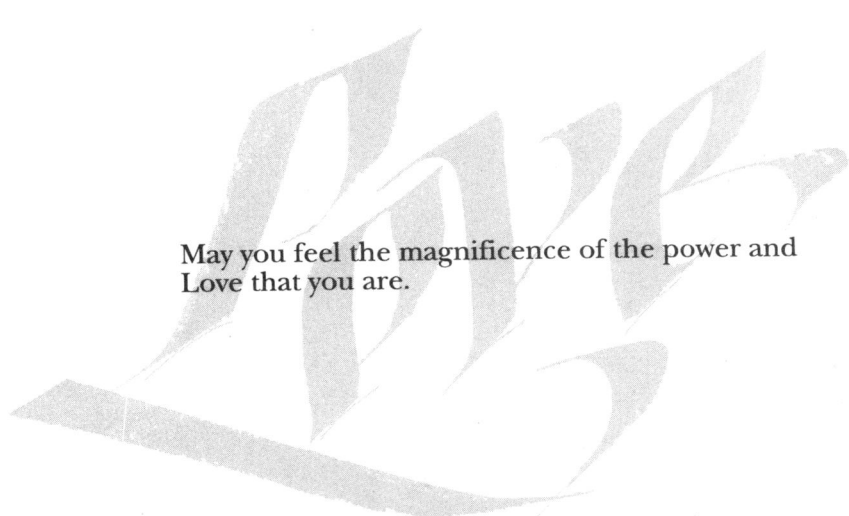

May you feel the magnificence of the power and Love that you are.

"I am with you
In that place
Where time
And space
Don't exist"
We are Love.

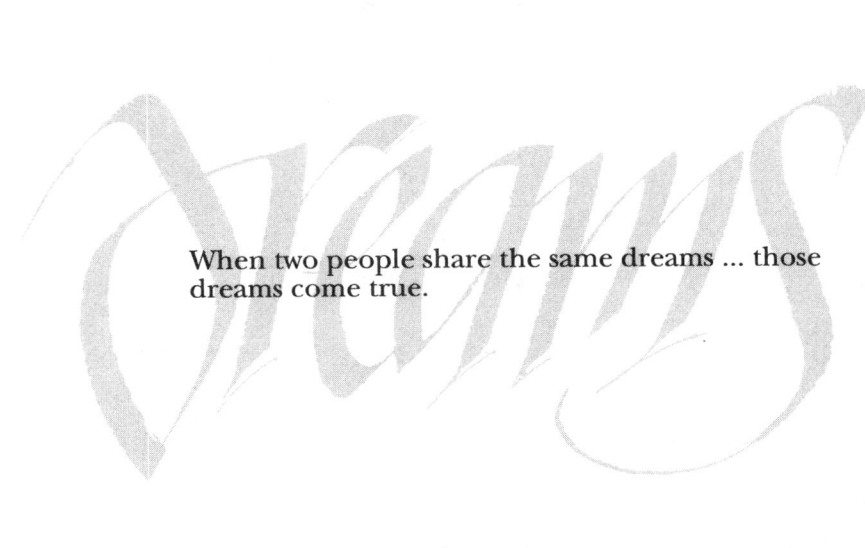

When two people share the same dreams ... those dreams come true.

When making Love becomes a sacrament ... a testimony to the Glory of God, we are in Heaven.

Play

My heart is your home, and my spirit plays in your garden.

Only Love is real, our relationship exists to serve God.

I am real
I am in you
And in your imagination
You are in me
And in my imagination

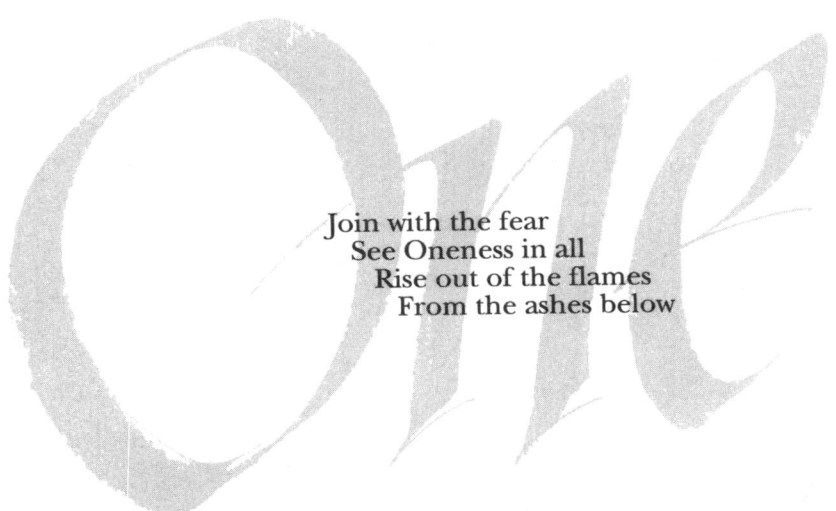

One

Join with the fear
See Oneness in all
Rise out of the flames
From the ashes below

I believe in you, my heart is with you. Know I am with you always.

I Love to touch you ... I touch to Love you.

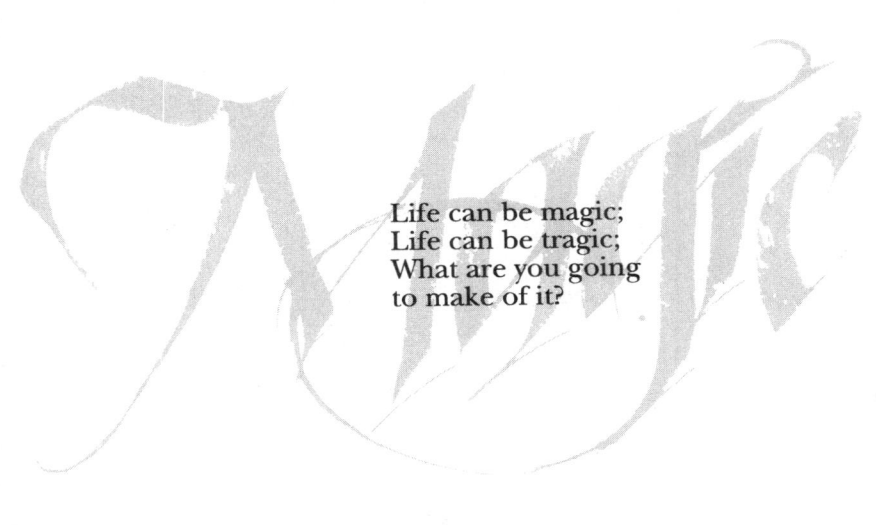

Life can be magic;
Life can be tragic;
What are you going
to make of it?

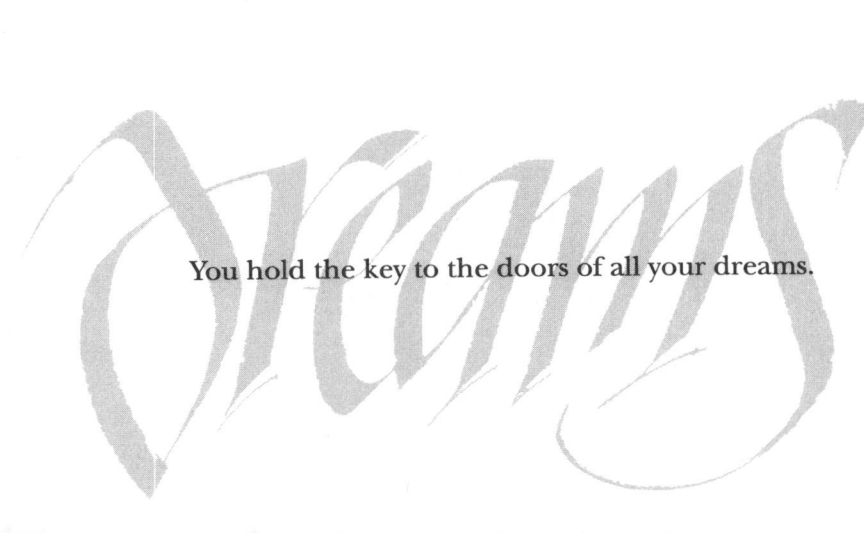

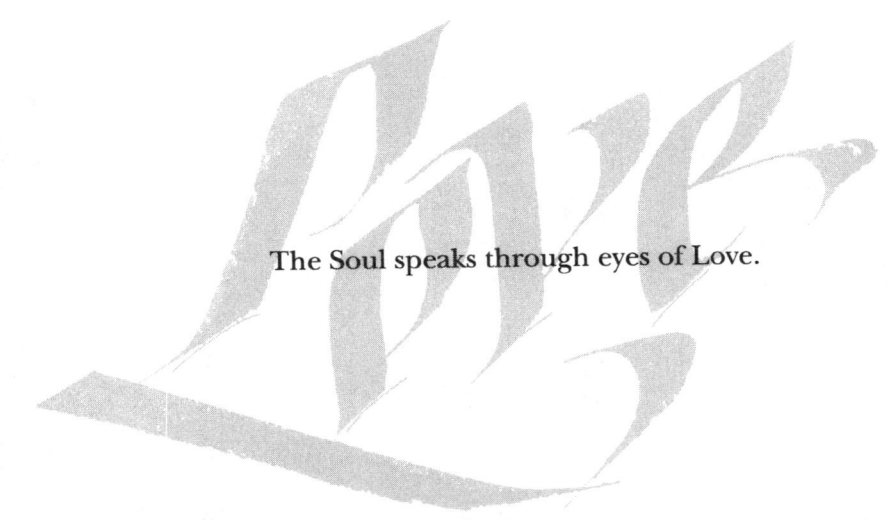

The Soul speaks through eyes of Love.

Light

Take my hand, walk beside me ... toward the Light beyond the sun.

One

With all creation, we are One.

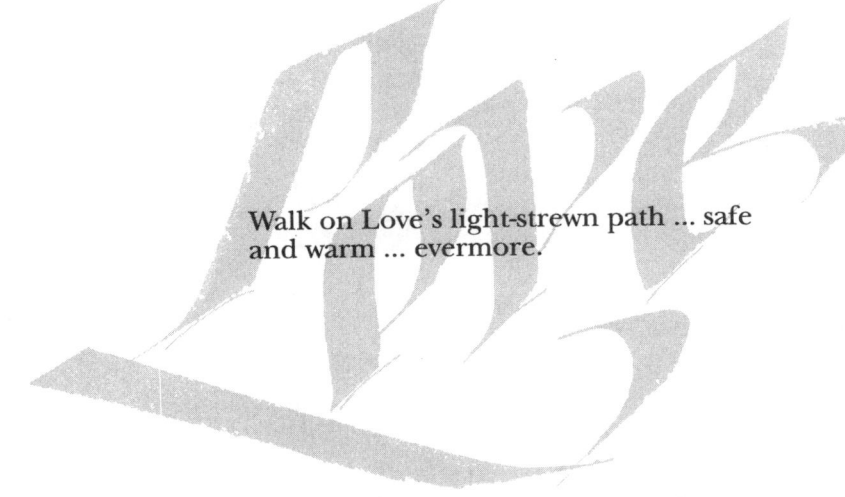

Walk on Love's light-strewn path ... safe and warm ... evermore.

One

In our minds ... in our hearts ... Love is fulfilled, we are One.

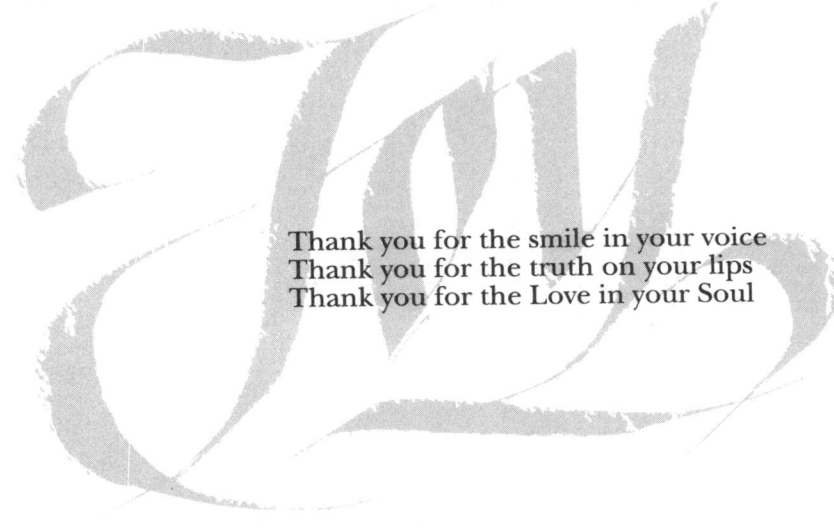

Thank you for the smile in your voice
Thank you for the truth on your lips
Thank you for the Love in your Soul

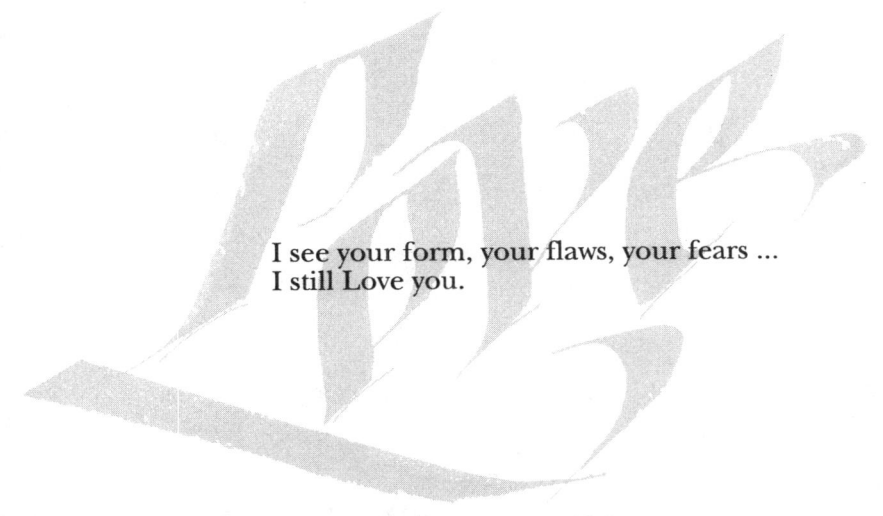

I see your form, your flaws, your fears ...
I still Love you.

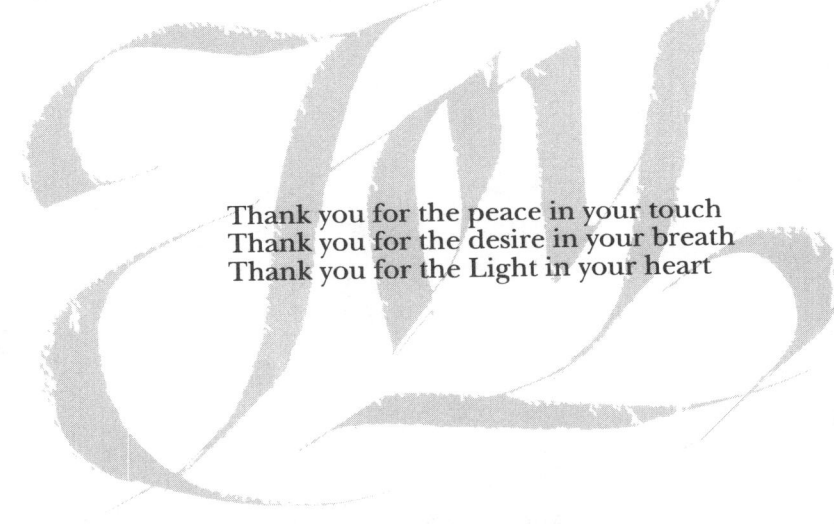

Thank you for the peace in your touch
Thank you for the desire in your breath
Thank you for the Light in your heart

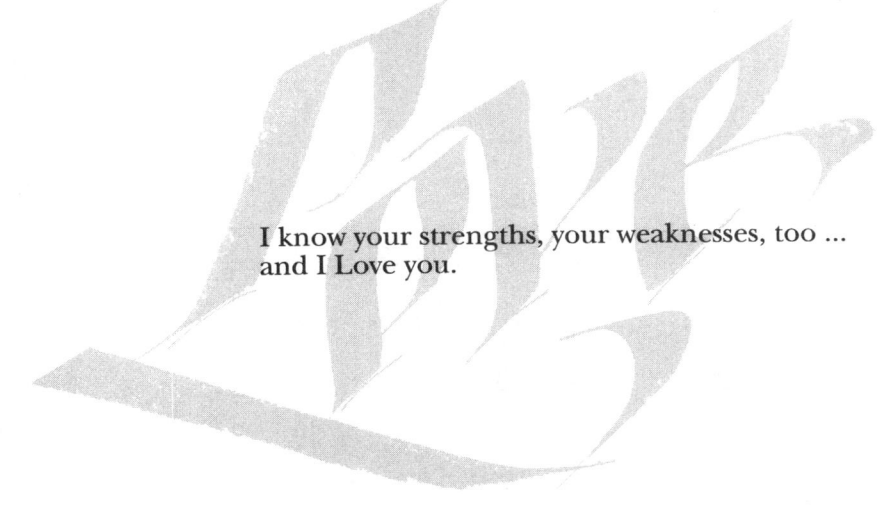

I know your strengths, your weaknesses, too ...
and I Love you.

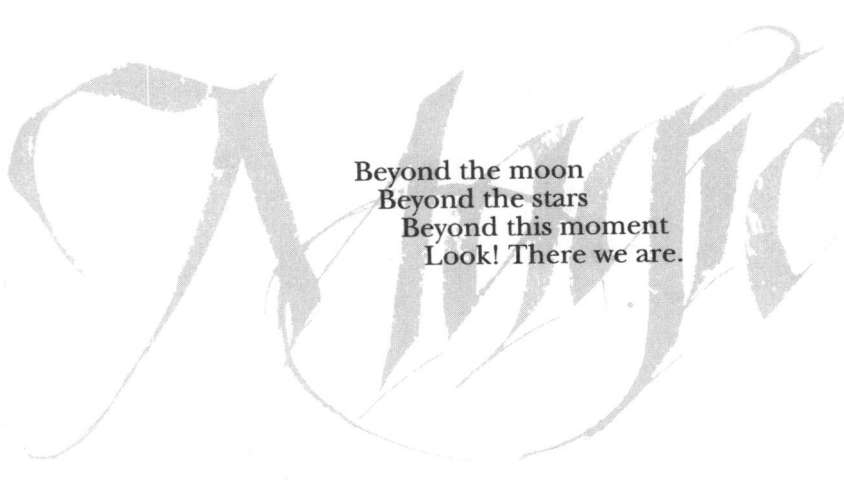

Beyond the moon
Beyond the stars
Beyond this moment
Look! There we are.

As I find my way, I light the way for others.

Love waits there where hearts are free.

Magical, mystical, miracle ... LOVE!

Web of Life
Catch my dreams
See them grow
My heart is Light
It now has wings

The truth of Love ... it never fails, though wander far we may.

Heart

Listen with your heart ... not your mind, your emotions, your body, your ears, your eyes.

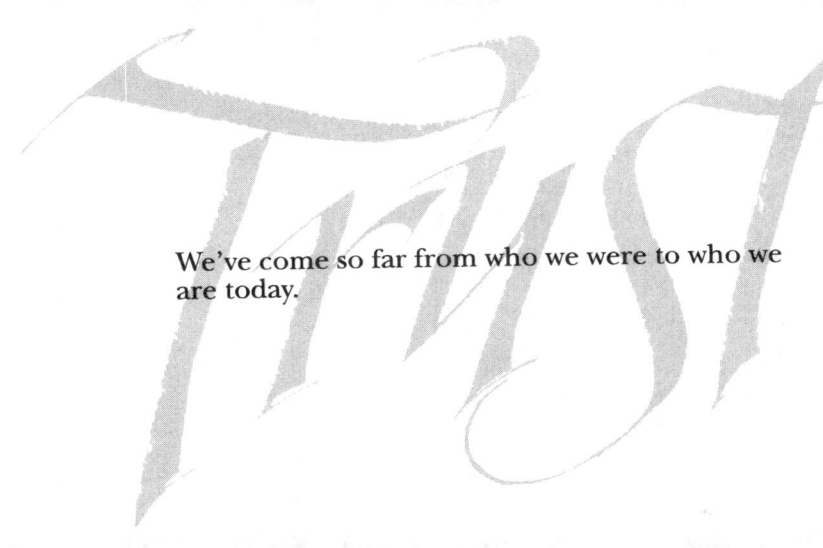

We've come so far from who we were to who we are today.

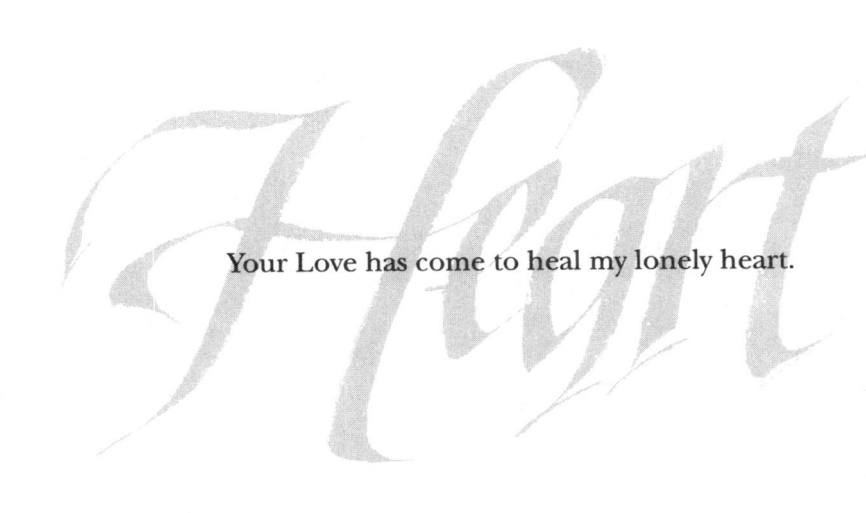

Your Love has come to heal my lonely heart.

Energy

Harness your sexual energy ... direct it toward creative efforts and you will change the world.

Love is a flower ... rejoice in the unfolding!

The sound of your voice touches my ears like Angels' voices speaking to my heart.

Peace

May we rest our wings beside the still waters of Your Love ... Home again.